Ricky Friesem   Naomi Moushine

Kosher

FRUITS OF THE EARTH

A HARVEST OF RECIPES
FROM THE LAND OF ISRAEL

Adama Books, New York

Illustrated by Rickie Lauffer

Library of Congress Cataloging-in-Publication Data

Friesem, Ricky.
   Fruits of the earth.
   Includes index.

   1. Cookery, Jewish. 2. Cookery – Israel. 3. Food
crops – Israel. I. Moushine, Naomi. II. Title.

TX724. F69   1985   641.5   85-13488

ISBN 0-915361-26-4

Adama Books, 306 West 38 Street, New York, N.Y. 10018

Printed in Israel

CONTENTS

Introduction

"...bless the Lord, thy God, for the good land which he hath given thee."

Deuteronomy 8:10

That it is a good land is not always obvious. The Land of the Bible often seems an inhospitable place, a land of rocks and deserts, of burning sun, parching winds and all too little water. A land where abundance cannot be taken for granted and where frequently an anxious eye is cast towards the heavens in anticipation of the first rains.

Perhaps because the land yields up its bounty so very grudgingly, the people of Israel have, from ancient times, attached such great importance to the fruits of the earth, greeting their appearance with special blessings, and song and joyous festivals.

For when the rains do come, and the winds cool, and the sun again shines, the Land of Israel can be extravagant in the variety of its riches. Milk and honey, wheat and barley, vines, figs, pomegranates, olives and dates. To this Biblical cornucopia Israel's remarkable agricultural revolution has added countless other species. Indeed recent experience has shown that there is very little which cannot be grown at this crossroads of the world.

It is this surprisingly abundant and variegated harvest — both ancient and modern — that has inspired the collection of recipes in this book.

שבעת
המינים

"...a land of wheat and
barley, and vines, and fig
trees, and pomegranates,
a land of olive and
honey."

Deuteronomy 8:8

THE SEVEN SPECIES

שבעת
המינים

THE SEVEN SPECIES

GOOD MORNING CEREAL

2 cups oats
1 cup brown sugar
1 cup chopped nuts (almonds or walnuts)
½ cup sesame seeds
½ cup chopped peanuts
½ cup sunflower seeds
(½ cup dried fruit and shredded coconut — optional)
1 Tb honey
½ cup water
1 cup raisins

Mix dry ingredients with honey and water solution. Spread evenly in pan and bake in hot oven for approximately 25 minutes. Cool. Add raisins. Store in closed containers.
For breakfast, mix 3 Tbs of cereal with milk or yoghurt.

OATMEAL SQUARES

2 cups oats
1 cup flour
1 cup sugar
1 cup shredded coconut
7 oz margarine
1 Tb honey
1 tsp bicarbonate of soda

Melt margarine with honey and soda on top of stove. Add remaining ingredients and mix thoroughly. Spread evenly on ungreased pan and press firmly. Bake in moderate oven for 20 minutes or until brown. Take pan out of oven and while still hot cut into squares. Cool. Break into squares and keep in airtight tin. Keeps indefinitely if not devoured.

TABOULI SALAD

½ lb fine burghul (cracked wheat)
3 Tbs finely chopped scallions
1½ cups finely chopped parsley
3 Tbs finely chopped fresh mint
or 2 Tbs dried crushed mint
1 lb finely chopped tomatoes
2 finely chopped cucumbers
4 Tbs olive oil
4 Tbs lemon juice
salt and pepper

The quantities can be varied according to taste, but the parsley should always dominate. Soak burghul in water for at least ½ hour before serving. It will expand enormously. Drain and squeeze out as much moisture as possible. Spread out to dry on a cloth.
Mix the burghul with the chopped onions, squeezing so that the onions will be crushed and their juice penetrate the burghul. Add parsley, mint, olive oil and lemon juice and mix well. Add salt, pepper.

RAISIN CAKE

3 cups unsifted flour
2 cups sugar
1 cup mayonnaise
⅓ cup milk
2 eggs
2 tsp baking soda
1½ tsp cinnamon
½ tsp nutmeg
½ tsp salt
¼ tsp cloves
3 cups peeled apples, chopped
1 cup raisins
½ cup chopped nuts

Grease and flour two 9″ round baking pans. In large bowl or mixer combine well first 10 ingredients. Batter will be very thick. Stir in apples, raisins and nuts. Spoon into 2 pans. Bake at 350° for 45 minutes. Cool in pans for 10 minutes and remove from oven. Fill and frost with 2 cups whipped cream.

GRAPES AND SOUR CREAM

2 lbs seedless grapes
1 cup sour cream
½ cup light brown sugar
grated orange rind

Wash and drain grapes. Remove stems. Combine with sour cream and sprinkle with brown sugar. Garnish with grated orange rind and chill at least 3 hours before serving.

FRESH GRAPE CAKE

7 oz margarine
5 eggs, separated
2½ cups flour (self rising)
½ tsp vanilla
1½ cups sugar
1 lb grapes (seedless or muscat)
¼ cup flour

Whip egg whites with ½ cup sugar until stiff. Beat yolks, margarine, sugar and vanilla until smooth. Add flour. Fold egg whites into flour mixture. Pour into a greased pan. Dust grapes with ¼ cup of flour. Arrange grapes on top of dough mixture. Bake in moderate oven for 40 minutes. Apples and raisins may be substituted for grapes.

WHITE GRAPE AND GINGER
AMBROSIA

2 lbs seedless white grapes, halved
2 cups crushed ginger cookies
4 egg whites, stiffly beaten
1 cup sugar
1¼ cups white wine
juice of ½ lemon
1⅞ cups heavy cream
1 cup slivered almonds, toasted

Arrange ¼ of the grapes on the bottom of a medium sized bowl. Cover with ¼ of the ginger cookie crumbs. Continue making layers until all the grapes and crumbs are used up. Set aside.
Place the beaten egg whites in medium sized mixing bowl. Beat in ¼ of the sugar. Using a metal spoon, fold in the remaining sugar. Add wine and lemon juice. Stir ingredients carefully until thoroughly combined. Set aside. Beat cream until it is thick but not stiff. Fold the egg white mixture into the cream. Then pour this mixture over the grape and cookie layers. Chill for 2 hours. Garnish with almonds and grapes.

BLACK AND WHITE SALAD

1 lb cooked chicken, diced
12 scallions, white part only, chopped
1 lb potatoes, peeled, cooked and diced
2 oz seedless raisins
8 oz large black grapes, halved and seeded
2 oz large black olives, halved and pitted
½ tsp salt
¼ tsp freshly ground black pepper
1 large apple, peeled, cored and diced
¾ cup mayonnaise

In a large bowl, combine the chicken, scallions, potatoes, raisins, half the grapes, olives, salt, pepper and apple. Add the mayonnaise and toss. Arrange the remaining grape halves decoratively over the top. Refrigerate for 30 minutes before serving.

FIG PARFAIT

½ cup chopped dried figs
¼ cup light brown sugar
½ cup water
¼ cup chopped walnuts
1 pint vanilla ice cream
whipped cream

Cook chopped figs, sugar and water until slightly thickened. Add chopped nuts and chill. Arrange alternating layers of ice cream and chilled fig sauce in parfait glasses. Top with whipped cream.

FIG COMPOTE

1 lb figs
½ cup sugar
juice of one lemon
2 cups water

Bring water and sugar to boil. Add whole figs (with skin). Boil for 15 minutes. Add lemon juice. Cool.

POMEGRANATE TREAT

seeds of 2 pomegranates
1 cup chopped nuts (almonds or peanuts)
¼ cup sugar
a few drops orange blossom water

Mix together and serve in glass to take full advantage of the color.

POMEGRANATES AND SOUR CREAM

seeds of 2 pomegranates
2 Tbs sugar
1 cup sour cream

Combine all ingredients. Serve cold.

SUMMER FRUIT SALAD

grapes (seedless)
plums
figs
melon or cantelope
watermelon
pomegranate
marsala wine, sugar, mint leaves

Cut all the fruit. Combine in large bowl. Pour marsala wine, sugar and mint leaves over fruit and toss. Cool in refrigerator.

OLIVE-RICE SALAD

4–5 cups cooked rice
1 sweet red pepper, chopped
1 cup pitted black olives
½ cup pitted green olives
1 green pepper, chopped
2 green onions, chopped
oil and vinegar dressing
salt and pepper to taste

Mix together all ingredients. Toss well with oil and vinegar dressing. Add salt and pepper to taste. Good hot or cold.

CHICKEN WITH ORANGES AND OLIVES

3 chicken breasts, halved
1 large onion, chopped
3 oranges, peeled and sliced
½ cup green olives, pitted
1 Tb flour
½ cup white or rosé wine
1−2 Tbs soy sauce, to taste
juice of one orange

Fry onions until transparent. Add chicken breasts and brown on both sides. Mix together orange juice, flour, wine, soy sauce and pour over chicken. Add orange slices and olives. Cook covered until meat is tender. Serve with rice.

COOKED OLIVES, MOROCCAN STYLE

2 lbs pitted olives
2 large ripe tomatoes
4–5 garlic cloves, peeled
¼ cup oil
¼ tsp cumin
½ tsp ground black pepper
juice of ½ a lemon
⅛ tsp hot paprika

Bring olives to boil in fresh water. Pour water out and repeat 2–3 times. Purée skinned tomatoes and sauté with oil until smooth. Add spices, chopped garlic and olives. Cook on low fire for about an hour. Add lemon juice.

HONEY PIE

2 cups apples or peaches, peeled and sliced
4 eggs
¾ cup honey
1 cup yoghurt
1 tsp vanilla
½ tsp cinnamon
¼ cup chopped walnuts

Line 9″ pie pan with pie dough or cookie crumbs. Spread fruit over pie shell. Combine remaining ingredients in blender and pour over apples. Sprinkle nuts on top. Bake 45 minutes, or until solid, in medium oven. Cool to room temperature before serving.

HONEY CAKE

1 cup sugar
1 cup honey
3 cups flour
2 eggs
5 Tbs oil
1 tsp baking soda
1 cup hot strong tea or coffee
raisins and nuts

Mix eggs with sugar, honey and flour. Add remaining ingredients and bake in greased pan for 45 minutes.

HONEY LEG OF LAMB

1 leg of lamb (about 5 or 6 lbs)
¼ cup honey
2 Tbs mustard
1 Tb brown sugar
salt and pepper to taste
1 orange sliced
1 lemon sliced

Cook lamb on rack in roasting pan at 300° for 2 hrs. Mix honey, mustard and brown sugar. Salt and pepper lamb. Pour mixture over meat and bake another 1–1½ hrs., or until done. Garnish with orange and lemon slices. Serve with mint jelly.

* Please note: to make this cut kosher, have you butcher remove the sciatic nerve.

DATE PARFAIT

½ cup chopped, pitted dates
1½ cups water
¼ cup sugar
4 egg yolks, well beaten
½ cup orange juice
½ cup heavy cream, whipped.

Cook dates in water for 20 minutes. Add sugar and cook 10 minutes longer. Pour slowly over egg yolks. In double boiler, cook over boiling water until thick, stirring constantly. Chill and add orange juice and whipped cream. Freeze until firm.

DATE-NUT TORTE

⅓ cup flour
1 tsp baking powder
¾ cup finely chopped nuts
3 eggs, separated
½ cup brown sugar
½ tsp vanilla
1 cup chopped dates
½ pint whipped cream

Beat egg whites until stiff. Beat yolks and sugar until thick. Add dry ingredients. Blend well. Mix in dates. Fold in egg whites. Bake at 350° for 50 minutes in 9″ round greased and floured pan. When cool, turn upside down on plate. Center will fall in slightly. Fill top with whipped cream.

DATE HORS D'OEUVRES

1 lb dates, pitted
almonds or pecan nuts
strips of smoked meat
tooth picks

Stuff each pitted date with almond or nut. Wind strip of meat around date and secure with tooth pick. Grill dates until meat is browned. Serve immediately.

DATE NIBBLES

1 cup pitted dates, finely diced
¼ cup honey
1½ cups creamed or chunky peanut butter
1 cup flaked coconut or sesame seeds, toasted

Mix together dates, honey and peanut butter, and shape into bite size balls. Roll in coconut or sesame seeds. Refrigerate several hours. Makes 3 dozen.

DATE AND NUT CAKE

1 lb dates, pitted
½ cup pecans or walnuts, chopped
1 cup sugar
1 cup self rising flour
4 eggs separated
⅛ cup brandy

Whip egg whites with 2 Tbs sugar until stiff. Gradually add yolks one at a time. Add the brandy. Mix dry ingredients − dates, sugar and chopped nuts. Fold egg white mixture into dry ingredients. Pour into greased square pan. Bake in moderate oven for 25 minutes, until top is golden brown. Cool, cut into squares.

DATE BARS

2 cups seedless dates
1½ cups Rice Krispies
3 Tbs sugar
5 oz butter or margarine

Break up dates. Put in pan on top of stove and melt together with butter and sugar. Add Rice Krispies. Remove from heat. Add 4 oz chopped walnuts and press mixture into greased pyrex or tin. Keep in refrigerator. Cut into squares.

STUFFED DATES

1 lb dates, pitted
ground coconut or sugar

Stuffing:
2 cups ground almonds
1 cup sugar
1 egg yolk

Mix ground almonds, sugar, egg yolk and cook over low fire until thick. Add 1 tsp water and cook for another minute. Cool. Stuff each date with filling and roll in coconut or sugar. Serve in individual fluted paper cups.

חצילים
וקישואים

ZUCCHINI ~ EGGPLANT

ZUCCHINI YOGHURT SALAD

1 cup plain yoghurt
2 Tbs olive oil
4 Tbs fresh mint
4 tsp lemon juice
2 cups zucchini, thinly sliced and peeled

Stir together first 4 ingredients. Add zucchini. Combine thoroughly. Chill.

"GEVETCH" (RATATOUILLE)

1 large onion, chopped
1 green pepper, cubed
2 zucchini, cubed
1 medium eggplant, cubed
2 large tomatoes, chopped
3—4 cloves garlic, crushed
¼ cup olive oil
2 Tbs tomato purée
½ cup tomato juice
½ tsp basil
½ tsp marjoram
½ tsp oregano
2 tsp salt
½ tsp ground black pepper
(cubes of spicy sausage may also be added)

Heat oil in heavy saucepan, add garlic and onion. Sauté until onion is transparent. Add vegetables, sausage, seasonings, tomato purée and juice. Cover and simmer until tender. Can be served with a topping of grated cheese.

ZUCCHINI PURÉE

3 medium zucchini
2 cups parve stock
¾ cup skim milk powder
1½ tsp salt
fresh black pepper
pinch of celery salt
½ tsp basil
1 cup chopped onion
¼ cup sour cream or yoghurt

Place zucchini, onion, water or stock and salt in saucepan and cook until zucchini is just tender. Purée in blender. Whisk in dry milk, sour cream and herbs. Heat until just hot enough to serve. Top with minced onions or chives.

COLD ZUCCHINI SOUP

4 medium zucchini, quartered and sliced
2 cups parve chicken broth
1 bunch scallions, chopped
1 tsp salt
1 tsp pepper
fresh dill to taste
8 oz cream cheese
1 cup sour cream
chopped chives or paprika for garnish

Cook zucchini, chicken broth, onions, salt, pepper and dill in saucepan until soft, about 20-30 minutes. Blend cream cheese and sour cream in blender or food processor and slowly add zucchini mixture until smooth. Chill until very cold. Garnish and serve.

STUFFED ZUCCHINI

2 lbs small zucchini
½ cup rice
1 lb ground meat
1 onion chopped
1 clove garlic, minced
salt, pepper, oregano and a little oil
4 oz tomato sauce
pinch of cinnamon

Scrape out inside of zucchini. Fry onions, garlic and inside of zucchini. Mix rice, meat and seasonings. Fill zucchini with meat and rice stuffing. Place zucchini on fried onion mixture. Cover with tomato sauce, season with oregano and a pinch of cinnamon. Cover and cook on top of stove. When ready transfer to baking dish and bake until tender. This recipe can be used for eggplants, green peppers and tomatoes.

ZUCCHINI IN TOMATO SAUCE

1 large onion
2 Tbs olive oil
2 Tbs oil
2 lb zucchini
4 oz tomato purée
½ cup water
1 Tbs powdered soup
1 clove garlic, crushed
2 Tbs chopped parsley
salt and pepper to taste

Fry chopped onion until golden. Add sliced zucchini, tomato purée mixed with water, seasonings and powdered soup. Bring to a boil, reduce heat and cook until tender. When cool, garnish with chopped parsley.

ZUCCHINI SOUFFLÉ

2 lbs zucchini
2 cups milk
2 Tbs flour
1 oz margarine
2 cups water
2 cups grated cheese
3 eggs
salt and pepper

Peel and cube zucchini. Boil, cool, drain, removing all liquid. Make sauce of milk, flour and margarine. Add grated cheese and beaten eggs. Take ¾ of sauce and mix with zucchini and pour in greased baking dish. Add remaining sauce and sprinkle a little more grated cheese on top. Dot with margarine. Bake.

MOCK ZUCCHINI LIVER

1 lb small zucchini
3 large onions, chopped
2 hard-boiled eggs
oil

Fry chopped onions, add sliced raw zucchini. Cover and cook over low fire, without adding water. When tender, mash with fork. Add pepper, salt and grated hard-boiled eggs. Serve cold.

EGGPLANT AND OLIVES

2 or 3 eggplants
2 Tbs margarine
2–3 Tbs flour
2 cups milk
salt and pepper
1 small onion, grated
½ cup black olives
½–1 cup grated cheese
mushroom soup powder

Peel, cut and boil eggplant until tender. Drain and mash. Make white sauce by mixing constantly flour, margarine, milk and a few spoonsful of mushroom soup powder in a saucepan over heat. Put eggplant in greased baking dish, cover with white sauce, decorate with olives and sprinkle cheese over top. Bake for 15–20 minutes.

EGGPLANT PIE

2 lbs of eggplant
1 onion
3−4 eggs
3 chopped onions
oil
grated cheese
pastry dough

Peel and cube eggplant. Boil together with the onion until tender. Drain thoroughly and mash. Fry chopped onion in oil until transparent. Add eggplant. Stir in beaten eggs and grated cheese. Do not cook for too long. Line baking dish with half of pastry, spread eggplant mixture, cover with rest of pastry. Brush egg yolk and a little milk over top. Prick top and bake until golden.

PICKLED EGGPLANT

2 lb small eggplants
2 cups water
1 Tb coarse salt
2 cups vinegar (preferably wine vinegar)
garlic cloves

Wash eggplants and slit on top. Put ½ garlic clove
in each slit. Boil in water, salt and vinegar mixture
until soft (not too soft!). Pour into jars and store
for a few days before serving.

PIQUANT EGGPLANT

1 large eggplant, sliced horizontally
2–3 cloves garlic, sliced
½ cup vinegar
¼–½ cup oil
¼ cup parsley

Slightly brown eggplant on both sides in very hot oil. Remove from frying pan and place on paper towel to drain off excess oil. Arrange slices in shallow serving dish. Pour vinegar over the slices. Add garlic and parsley. Chill in refrigerator for several hours before serving. Keeps for days.

EGGPLANT CASSEROLE

1 large eggplant
1 onion, chopped
1 tomato, peeled, seeded and chopped
½ cup chopped celery
1 egg, beaten
8 black olives, pitted and sliced
6 anchovies, diced
¾ cup soft bread crumbs
½ cup parmesan cheese
salt and pepper

Peel and cube eggplant and steam or parboil for 5−10 mintues. Drain and add remaining vegetables, eggs, olives, anchovies, seasoning and half the bread crumbs. Pour into greased baking dish and top with remaining crumbs and cheese. Bake at 325° for 30 minutes.

EGGPLANT SPREAD*

1 medium eggplant
3 Tbs minced onion
2 Tbs salad or olive oil
4 Tbs lemon juice
1½ tsp salt
¼ tsp pepper
1 tsp sugar

Bake eggplant in 475° oven until skin is scorched.
Cool and peel. Chop eggplant until very smooth.
Stir in the onion, oil, lemon juice, salt, pepper and
sugar. Chill. Serve with dark bread and wedges of
tomatoes.

* "Tahina" (sesame seed paste) may be added to this spread
to taste.

עגבניות ~ אבוקדו

TOMATOES ~ AVOCADOS

CHILLED TOMATO SOUP

1 chopped cucumber
1 chopped scallion
1 clove crushed garlic
1 tsp honey
½ tsp dill
4 cups tomato juice
1 cup yoghurt
1 chopped green pepper
several fresh raw mushrooms
Salt and pepper

Combine and chill. Serve with croutons. Garnish
with dill. Serves 4 to 6.

PIQUANT TOMATO SOUP

½ pint tomato juice
½ pint chicken stock
1 tsp celery salt
1 crushed garlic clove
½ bunch of watercress
6 large spinach leaves
finely chopped mint

Mix tomato juice with chicken stock. Add powdered celery salt and crushed garlic. In blender or processor, purée watercress with a little of the tomato-chicken mixture and spinach leaves until smooth. Stir in remaining mixture. Chill well before serving. Decorate with chopped mint leaves.

STUFFED TUNA TOMATOES

4 tomatoes, halved and seeded
1 hard boiled egg
1 can tuna
2 scallions chopped
½ tsp salt
¼ tsp pepper
1 Tb mayonnaise
1 Tb vinegar

In a bowl, mix well hard boiled egg, tuna, scallions. Add seasonings. Spoon mixture into tomatoes, chill and serve.

BRANDY TOMATO SALAD

2 lbs tomatoes
3 onions
garlic
1 Tb chicken soup powder
paprika
3 Tbs ketchup
2 Tbs brandy
2 Tbs chopped parsley

Fry chopped onions and garlic lightly in a little oil. Add cubed tomatoes, soup powder, salt and pepper. Stew slowly until cooked. Remove from heat. Add a few fresh chopped green onions, parsley, ketchup and brandy.

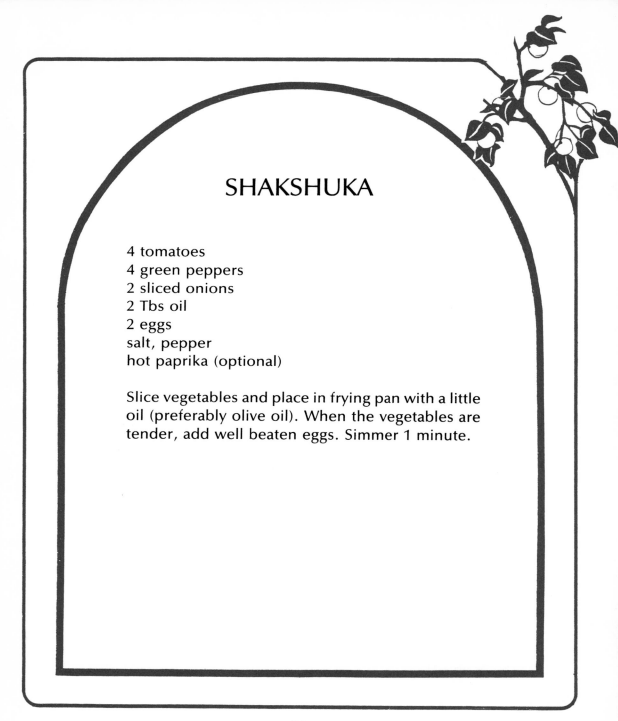

SHAKSHUKA

4 tomatoes
4 green peppers
2 sliced onions
2 Tbs oil
2 eggs
salt, pepper
hot paprika (optional)

Slice vegetables and place in frying pan with a little oil (preferably olive oil). When the vegetables are tender, add well beaten eggs. Simmer 1 minute.

AVOCADO DESSERT

2 ripe avocados
½ cup fresh lemon juice
6 Tbs confectioner's sugar
4 slices of citrus fruit for garnish

Mix the avocado with the sugar and lemon juice (in blender or food processor). Serve very cold, garnished with a slice of citrus fruit. Serves 4.

AVOCADO APPETIZER

2 avocados, halved and pitted

sauce vinaigrette:
mustard
salt
pepper
oil
vinegar

Pour the sauce into avocados. Eat with dessert spoon and enjoy.

CHILLED AVOCADO SOUP

2 ripe avocados
2 tsp lemon juice
1 celery stalk, finely chopped
1 Tb tomato purée
1 pint yoghurt (unsweetened)
salt and freshly ground black pepper
2 cups chicken stock
a dash of tabasco
chives for garnish

Halve the avocados and scoop the flesh into a bowl. Add the lemon juice and mash with fork until smooth. Stir in remaining ingredients, adding enough stock to make a pouring consistency. Chill well for 30 minutes in bowl of ice cubes. Serve garnished with chives. Do not leave the soup longer than 1 hour after mixing because the avocados will cause it to discolor.

גזרים ~ מלפפונים

CARROTS~CUKES

CUCUMBER SALAD

3 cucumbers, peeled and sliced
1 tsp salt
1 tsp dill weed
⅓ cup vinegar
1 tsp sugar
2 Tbs water
⅛ tsp pepper
2 diced scallions

Put peeled and sliced cucumbers in bowl. Sprinkle with salt. Set aside for 20 minutes. Drain well. Mix together remaining ingredients and add to the cucumbers. Mix well and refrigerate for at least 2 hours before serving. Will keep several days in the refrigerator.

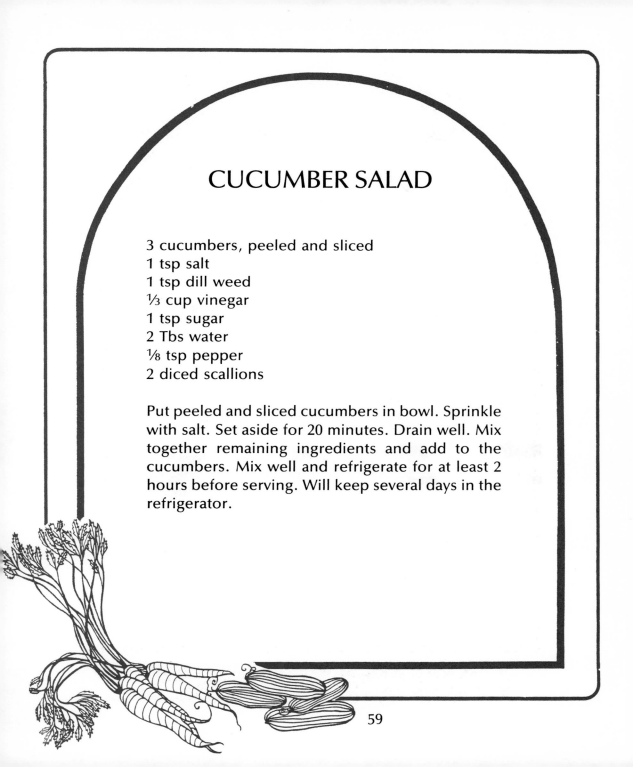

COLD CUCUMBER
BUTTERMILK SOUP

5 cucumbers
½ cup chopped parsley
6 scallions, chopped
2 Tbs freshly chopped dill
¼ cup lemon juice
1 quart buttermilk
1 pint sour cream (optional)
salt and freshly ground white pepper

garnish: ½ cup finely chopped radishes, ½ cup cucumbers, finely cubed, or fresh mint leaves.

Peel cucumbers, cut in half and remove seeds. Sprinkle with salt and let stand for 30 minutes. Drain. Cut cucumbers into chunks and put in blender with parsley, scallions, dill, lemon juice, buttermilk and sour cream. Blend at high speed. Add salt and pepper and chill well. Garnish before serving.

CUCUMBER POTATO SOUP

1 bunch scallions, chopped
2 Tbs butter
4 cups diced cucumber
3 cups parve chicken broth
1 cup chopped fresh spinach
½ cup sliced peeled potatoes
½ tsp salt; pepper to taste
1 Tb lemon juice
1 cup light cream

Sauté onions in butter until soft. Add cucumbers, chicken broth, spinach, potatoes, salt, lemon juice and pepper. Simmer uncovered until potatoes are tender. Transfer to blender or food processor in batches and purée. Pour into large bowl and stir in light cream. Refrigerate for several hours.

COOKED CUCUMBERS

1 dozen fresh little cucumbers
butter
grated cheese
bread crumbs

Peel and halve the cucumbers. Drop into boiling salted water and cook barely 5 minutes. Drain and place halves, flat side down in a buttered baking dish. Sprinkle with grated cheese and bread crumbs. Put under broiler until top is brown. Serve hot.

COLD YOGHURT SOUP
FOR A HOT DAY

3 cups yoghurt
3 cucumbers, chopped
1 cup water
½ cup chopped almonds
2 chopped pickles
½ cup raisins
2 oz salty white cheese, finely mashed
chopped dill or mint leaves

Mix all ingredients. Cool in refrigerator. If mixture is too thick add water. Before serving add ice cubes.

PICKLED CUCUMBERS

2—4 lbs small cucumbers
dill
10 garlic cloves
salt, water

In bottom of large jar, put dill and 4—5 garlic cloves. Pack small cucumbers tightly in jar. Cover with water. For each cup of water, add 1 Tb of coarse salt. Cover the solution with more dill and garlic. Cover with a heavy lid (so that no air will enter). Put the jar in the sun until the color of the cucumbers changes.

CARROT BURGERS

1 lb carrots
¼ cup flour
salt
butter
3 eggs, beaten
½ cup chopped walnuts
pepper

Wash and grate carrots. Add beaten eggs, flour, salt and pepper to taste. Melt butter in large frying pan and drop carrot mixture by tablespoons into greased pan. Flatten like a little cake and turn when nicely browned. Serve immediately. Serves 6.

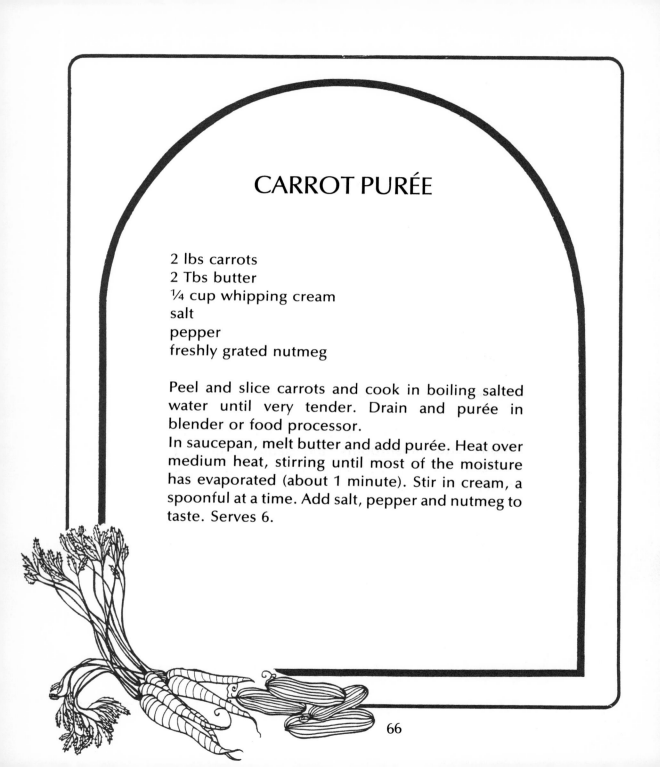

CARROT PURÉE

2 lbs carrots
2 Tbs butter
¼ cup whipping cream
salt
pepper
freshly grated nutmeg

Peel and slice carrots and cook in boiling salted water until very tender. Drain and purée in blender or food processor.
In saucepan, melt butter and add purée. Heat over medium heat, stirring until most of the moisture has evaporated (about 1 minute). Stir in cream, a spoonful at a time. Add salt, pepper and nutmeg to taste. Serves 6.

CARROT LOAF

4½ cups grated carrots
1 lb chopped mushrooms
5 eggs
2 cloves garlic
1 cup chopped onions
1 cup whole wheat bread crumbs
1 cup grated cheddar
¼ cup butter
salt, pepper, basil, thyme

Crush garlic into melting butter in frying pan. Add onions and mushrooms and sauté until soft. Combine all ingredients but save half the bread crumbs and cheese. Season to taste.
Spread into buttered oblong baking pan. Sprinkle with remaining bread crumbs and cheese. Dot with butter. Bake at 350°, 30 minutes covered and 5 minutes uncovered.

CARROT SALAD

¾ cup grated carrots
1 large apple
1 Tb lemon juice
¼ cup mayonnaise
¼ tsp salt
¼ cup raisins

Grate carrots and apple and add lemon juice immediately. Add other ingredients. Toss. Cool before serving.

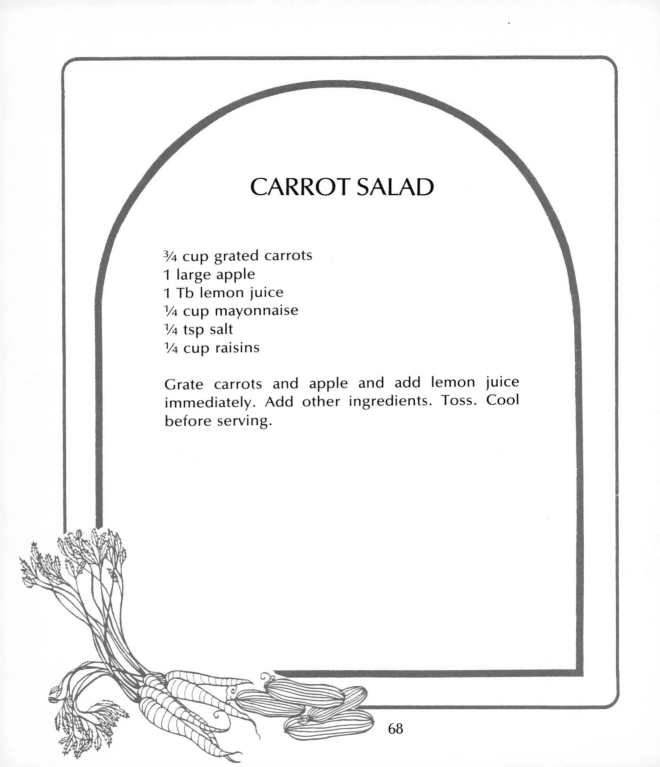

CARROT CAKE

1½ cups oil
2 cups sugar (1 white, 1 brown)
2 cups grated carrots
4 eggs
2 cups regular flour
1 tsp cinnamon
2 tsp baking powder
1 cup chopped nuts
1 cup crushed pineapple (drained)
shredded coconut

Mix all ingredients together well. Divide into 3 pans. Bake at 350° for 30 minutes or until done.

Icing:
½ package icing sugar, or more, depending on taste
2 oz margarine or butter
½ large package cream cheese
Blend well and spread evenly.

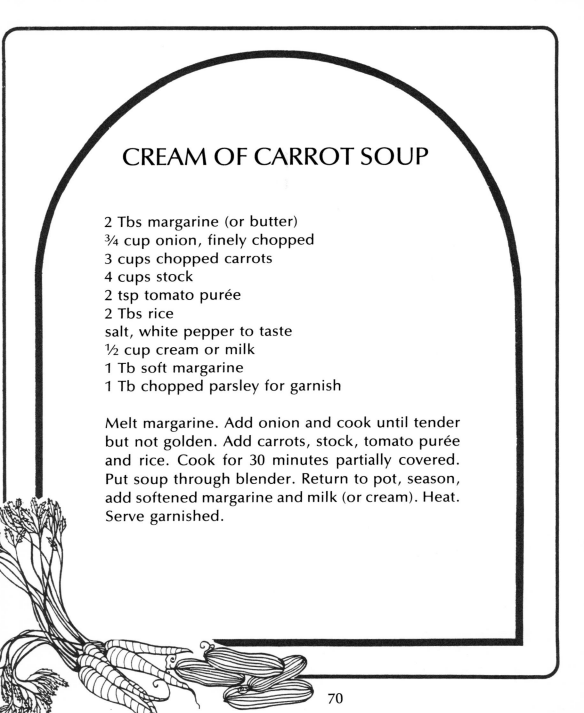

CREAM OF CARROT SOUP

2 Tbs margarine (or butter)
¾ cup onion, finely chopped
3 cups chopped carrots
4 cups stock
2 tsp tomato purée
2 Tbs rice
salt, white pepper to taste
½ cup cream or milk
1 Tb soft margarine
1 Tb chopped parsley for garnish

Melt margarine. Add onion and cook until tender but not golden. Add carrots, stock, tomato purée and rice. Cook for 30 minutes partially covered. Put soup through blender. Return to pot, season, add softened margarine and milk (or cream). Heat. Serve garnished.

CARROTS AND ONIONS
WITH RAISINS IN WINE

2 oz butter
1 lb carrots, cut into slices
8 oz small white onions, peeled and left whole
4 oz seedless raisins
1 tsp salt
½ tsp black pepper
¼ tsp cayenne pepper
1 tsp dried thyme
1 bay leaf
½ cup medium dry white wine
¼ cup heavy cream

In a large sauce pan, melt butter. Add carrots, onions and raisins. Cook them, stirring constantly for 4 minutes. Add seasonings, pour in wine. Cover the pan and simmer over low fire for 45–50 minutes or until vegetables are tender. Remove the pan from the heat and discard the bay leaf. Stir in the cream. Return to a very low heat for 1–2 minutes to warm the sauce slightly. Turn into a serving dish. Serve immediately.

ISRAELI SALAD

1 carrot
2 tomatoes
1 cucumber
2 radishes
2 pickled cucumbers
2 scallions
2 Tbs olive oil
juice of one lemon
1 tsp salt
pepper

Cut all vegetables into small pieces. Add seasonings and toss.

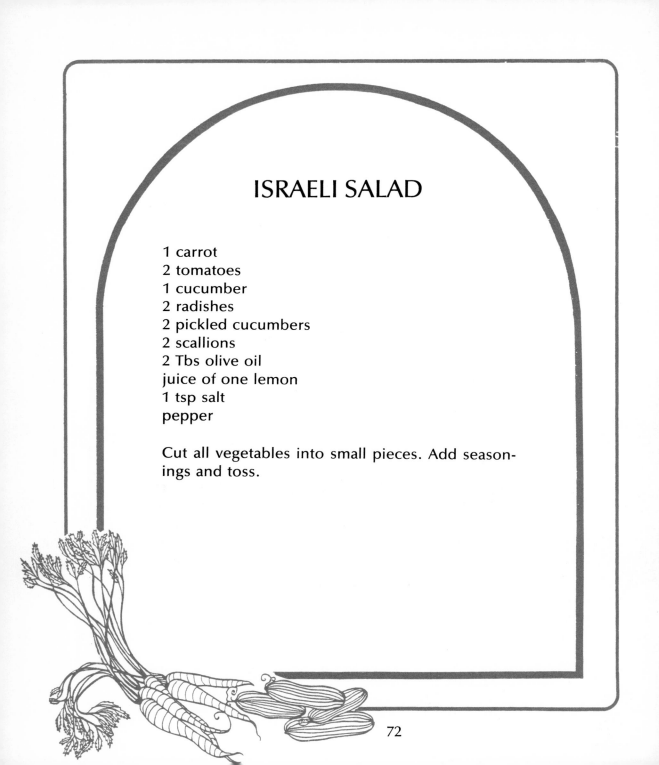

"TSIMMES"

8 carrots (medium size)
3 Tbs margarine
½ tsp salt
1 cup water
½ cup prunes
4 Tbs sugar (preferably brown)
½ tsp cinnamon
¼ tsp cloves
1 Tb lemon juice
2 Tbs chopped, candied orange peel
2 Tbs honey

Melt margarine in pan. Add sliced carrots and cook for 1–2 minutes (carrots do not have to brown). Add water and sugar and bring to boil. Add rest of ingredients and cook covered on low fire for approximately 2 hours. After 2 hours, remove lid and cook for 20 minutes until liquid becomes glazed. Serve.

CARROT SOUP

2 lbs carrots
4 cups stock or water
1½ tsp salt
1 medium potato
1 cup chopped onion
1−2 small cloves crushed garlic
⅓ cup chopped cashews or almonds

Boil carrots, water, salt and potato. Cover and simmer for 12−15 minutes. Let cool to room temperature. Sauté onion, garlic and chopped cashews or almonds in 3−4 Tbs butter with a little salt until onions are clear. Purée everything except cashews in a blender until smooth. Return to double boiler and whisk in only one of the following:
1 cup milk
1 cup yoghurt or buttermilk
½ pint whipping cream
¾ cup sour cream
Heat very slowly. Nutmeg, mint and cinnamon seasoning, optional. Garnish with sour cream and cashews.

פרי הדר

CITRUS

ORANGE PEEL

For every cup of peel:
¾ cup sugar
½ cup water

Quarter and peel oranges and soak the peel in water for 2—3 days. Change the water several times. Boil the peel in fresh water for 20 minutes. Strain. Cut in strips. For every cup of peel, add ¾ cup sugar and ½ cup water. Bring to boil and simmer on very low heat for a few hours until most of the liquid disappears. Arrange the peel on a cookie sheet or paper towel to dry for a few days. Roll in sugar and store in tightly closed jar.

ORANGE CAKE

2 cups self rising flour
4 eggs
1¼ cups sugar
½ cup orange juice
grated peel of 2 oranges
½ cup oil

Separate eggs. Mix sugar and yolks. Add oil. Add flour, juice alternately. Add grated peel. Mix together. Beat egg whites until stiff and add slowly. Bake ¾ of an hour in medium oven.

Icing:
2 squares unsweetened chocolate
3 Tbs margarine
2½ cups icing sugar
1 egg
Melt together in double boiler. Cool slightly and spread evenly on cake.

ORANGE ONION SALAD

4 large oranges
1 Spanish onion, thinly sliced
4 cups shredded lettuce
1 Tb chopped parsley
chopped walnuts (optional)

Dressing:
⅓ cup orange juice
½ tsp dried mustard
1 tsp salt
freshly ground pepper to taste
½ cup oil
½ tsp sugar

To prepare dressing, place all ingredients except the oil in jar and shake well to mix. Add oil and shake until blended. Peel the oranges and remove all the white pith. Cut into ⅛" slices and place in bowl. Toss the onions and oranges together. Add dressing. Garnish with parsley or chopped nuts.

ORANGE COOKIES

2 cups flour
2 tsp baking powder
¼ tsp salt
⅔ cup butter or margarine
¾ cup sugar
1 egg
grated peel of 2 oranges
3 Tbs freshly squeezed orange juice
chopped nuts, coconut, cinnamon, sugar

Sift together flour, baking powder and salt. Cream together butter and sugar. Add egg, orange peel and juice. Beat well. Gradually blend in dry ingredients. Chill 1 hour or more. Shape dough into 1″ balls. Place on ungreased cookie sheets. Sprinkle with nuts, coconut, sugar and cinnamon. Bake at 350° for 12−15 minutes. Makes 3 dozen.

ORANGE FRAPPÉ

¼ cup orange juice
1 scoop chocolate ice cream
1 cup cold milk
1 orange, sliced
1 Tb sugar

Beat ice cream with sugar and orange juice. Add milk and whip. Serve in tall glass with orange slice.

BEETS IN ORANGE SAUCE

2–2½ cups diced cooked or canned beets
1 Tb butter
¼ cup brown sugar
1½ Tbs flour
¾ cup orange juice
1 Tb grated orange peel
salt, paprika

Melt butter. Add brown sugar, flour, orange juice and grated peel. Cook until thick, stirring constantly. Season with salt and paprika. Add beets and heat.

ORANGE AND LEMON GLAZED CHICKEN

1 cup orange juice
¼ cup lemon juice
2 Tbs grated orange rind
1 cup light brown sugar
1¼ tsp dry mustard
¼ tsp allspice
3½−4 lb chicken, quartered
2 oranges, sliced

Arrange chicken in baking dish. Heat and blend remaining ingredients, except orange slices and pour over chicken. Bake at 375° for 1−1½ hours, until tender, basting frequently. Garnish with orange slices and serve.

EASY MARMALADE

6 oranges
3 lemons
7½ cups water
10 cups sugar

Wash fruit, cut in half lengthwise and slice very
thinly. Remove seeds before slicing. Put fruit in
large bowl and cover with water. Allow to stand
overnight. Put fruit and the same water in saucepan, bring to boil and reduce heat. Cover and
simmer for 40 minutes. Add sugar and stir over low
heat until dissolved. Bring to boil and cook rapidly
uncovered for 45−55 minutes. Start testing after 40
minutes. Remove skim. Cool slightly, bottle.
Makes about 6 jars.

ORANGE AND AVOCADO SALAD

2 oranges, sliced
1 avocado, cut into pieces
salt, pepper
oil
lemon juice

Mix slices of orange with avocado. Season.

CHICKEN WITH ORANGE SAUCE

one 2½–3 lb chicken, cut in serving pieces
1 tsp salt
¼ cup parve margarine
2 Tbs flour
2 Tbs sugar
½ tsp cinnamon
dash ginger
1½ cups orange juice
½ cup raisins
½ cup flaked coconut
hot cooked rice

Brown seasoned chicken in margarine. Remove from pan. Add flour, sugar, spices to drippings. Mix to paste. Add orange juice gradually. Cook, stirring till thickened. Add chicken and raisins. Cover and simmer for 40 minutes, or until done. Place on serving dish, sprinkle with coconut. Serve with rice and minted green peas. (When cooking peas, add few sprigs of mint, half a tsp sugar, salt and pepper to taste).

LEMON CRUMB SQUARES

1½ cups sifted flour
1 tsp baking powder
½ tsp salt
1 cup oatmeal
1 cup tightly packed brown sugar
½ cup butter

Filling:
15 oz can sweetened condensed milk
½ cup lemon juice, lemon rind

Combine condensed milk, lemon juice and rind. Sift together flour and baking powder. Cream butter and sugar. Add oatmeal, salt and flour mixture. Mix until crumbly.
Spread ⅔ dry mixture into 9″ greased pan. Pack down well. Pour in filling. Top with remaining crumbly mixture. Bake at 350° for 25–30 minutes. Cool and cut into 3″ squares.

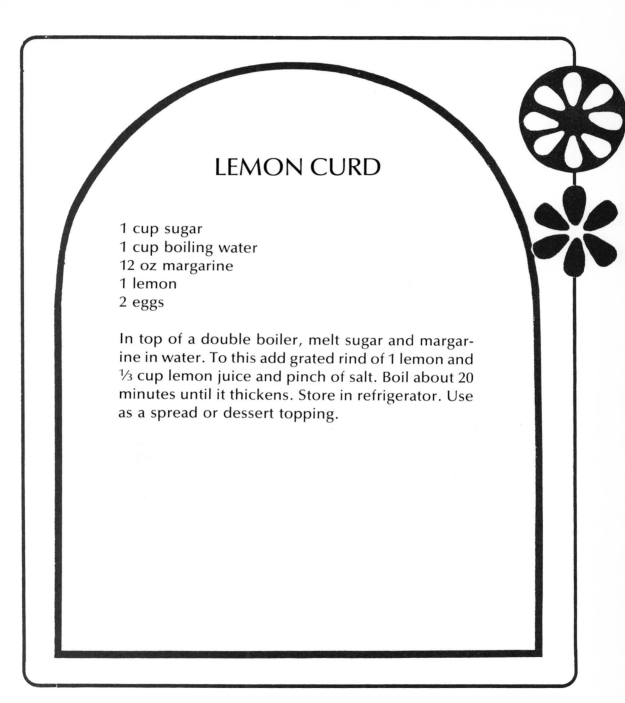

LEMON CURD

1 cup sugar
1 cup boiling water
12 oz margarine
1 lemon
2 eggs

In top of a double boiler, melt sugar and margarine in water. To this add grated rind of 1 lemon and ⅓ cup lemon juice and pinch of salt. Boil about 20 minutes until it thickens. Store in refrigerator. Use as a spread or dessert topping.

LEMON BAVARIA

juice of 2 lemons
rind of 2 lemons
4 eggs, separated
½ cup sugar
½ envelope unflavored gelatine diluted in ¼ cup water
1 cup whipping cream, whipped
(oranges may be used instead of the lemons in this recipe)

Mix over double boiler, juice of two lemons, rind, egg yolks, sugar and gelatine until smooth (if you prefer a more lemony taste add more rind). Cool. Fold in stiffly beaten egg whites and whipped cream. Pour into separate serving dishes or into one serving bowl. Refrigerate until firm.

GRILLED GRAPEFRUIT

3 grapefruits
6 Tbs sugar or honey
3 Tbs margarine or butter
cherries and mint leaves (optional)

Cut the fruit in half, remove the core and loosen each section. Fill the center with butter and sprinkle the fruit with sugar or honey. Grill until golden under a medium flame. Serve hot with a cherry or a spring of mint.

GRAPEFRUIT AND WINE MOUSSE

1 cup grapefruit juice
1 cup white wine (dry)
¾ cup sugar
4 eggs separated
2 Tbs cornflour

Mix grapefruit juice, wine, ½ cup sugar, egg yolks and cornflour. Bring to boil, stirring constantly. When it thickens, turn off heat and cool. Whip egg whites and ¼ cup of sugar until stiff. Fold egg whites into cool grapefruit mixture. Refrigerate. Garnish with cherry or mint leaves.

הַשְּׁמֵשִׁים • אַפְרְסְקִים • תּוּת־שָׂדֶה

APRICOTS, PEACHES,
STRAWBERRIES

APRICOT RICE MOLD

1 can apricot halves
1¼ tsp unflavored gelatine
2 cups cold cooked rice
½ cup heavy cream, whipped

Drain apricots and place half an apricot in each custard cup. Press remaining halves through a sieve. Soften gelatine in 3 Tbs apricot juice and dissolve over hot water. Combine dissolved gelatine, rice and puréed apricots and mix well. Fold in whipped cream and pour into custard cups. Chill. When firm, unmold and garnish with whipped cream.

APRICOT TONGUE

whole tongue
4 cups water
¾ cup white raisins
½ lb dried apricots

Boil tongue and cool. Remove skin. Slice and place in greased pan. Meanwhile, add water to dried apricots and cook until soft. Drain water and put aside. Strain apricots and add to the raisins and sugar. Pour apricot water back into fruit mixture and cook until slightly thick. Pour over sliced tongue and heat in 325° oven for ½ hour.

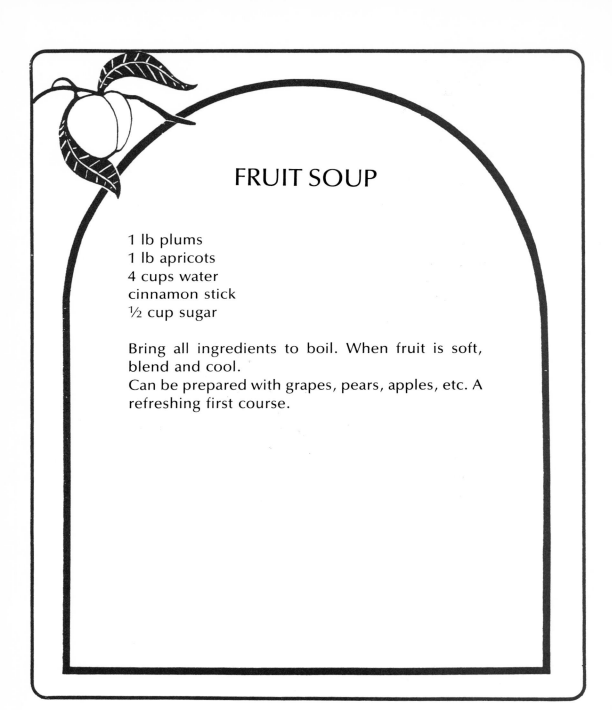

FRUIT SOUP

1 lb plums
1 lb apricots
4 cups water
cinnamon stick
½ cup sugar

Bring all ingredients to boil. When fruit is soft, blend and cool.
Can be prepared with grapes, pears, apples, etc. A refreshing first course.

PEACH BAVARIAN CREAM

1½ cups chopped fresh peaches
2 Tbs lemon juice
⅔ cup sugar
1½ Tbs unflavored gelatine
½ cup water
1 cup heavy cream, whipped
1 tsp vanilla

Combine peaches, lemon juice and sugar. Let stand 1 hour. Soften gelatine in cold water and then dissolve over low heat. Combine with peach mixture and chill. When mixture begins to thicken, fold in whipped cream and vanilla. Place in individual dessert cups and chill until firm. Garnish with peach slices or whipped cream.

PEACHY DESSERT

4 fresh peaches, peeled, halved and pitted
3 Tbs whipping cream
1 Tb sugar
1 tsp vanilla essence
1 oz dark chocolate, finely grated
4 Tbs blanched, slivered almonds

Arrange 2 peach halves, rounded sides down in each of 4 individual dessert dishes. Set aside. In a medium sized mixing bowl, whisk the cream, sugar and vanilla essence together until the mixture forms soft peaks. With a spoon or spatula, gently fold half of the chocolate and half of the almonds into the cream mixture. Place a little of the mixture in each peach half. Sprinkle each dish with equal amounts of the remaining grated chocolate and almonds. Chill 1 hour before serving.

JELLO FRUIT CAKE

1½ cups self rising flour
¼ cup sugar
1 egg yolk
5 oz margarine
1½ packages instant jello (strawberry, apricot, or any other flavor)
1 lb fruit (strawberries, apricots, grapes, etc.)

Mix flour, sugar, margarine and egg yolk. Spread on a greased spring pan and bake until the dough is golden, in a moderate oven. Cool. Arrange on cool dough the fruit of your choice. Prepare jello according to instructions and pour over fruit. Cool until firm. Garnish with whipped cream.

PEACH GLAZED CORNED BEEF

1 lean corned beef (about 4 lbs)
1 large can peach halves
¼ cup peach syrup
¼ cup brown sugar
2 Tbs vinegar
¼ cup ketchup
2 Tbs prepared mustard

Cover and simmer corned beef slowly in enough water to cover, about 3—4 hours or until tender. Remove meat and allow to cool. Slice across grain and arrange in overlapping slices in flat baking dish. Top with peaches. Mix peach syrup, brown sugar and vinegar. Add ketchup and mustard. Pour over meat. Bake in 350° oven, about 1 hour, basting often.

CHICKEN BREASTS
WITH PEACHES OR APRICOTS

2 whole chicken breasts cut into 2, brushed with
juice of one lemon
1 can peaches/or apricots
4 Tbs flour
1 tsp curry powder
1 tsp salt
½ tsp black pepper

Sauce:
1 onion, chopped
1 Tb soya sauce
juice from canned fruit
2 Tbs lemon juice

Mix dry ingredients and dredge breasts in mixture.
Fry until brown on both sides. Put each piece in
baking dish with a peach or apricot half on top.
Prepare sauce, pour over chicken breasts and
marinate overnight. Bake ½ hour in a moderate
oven and serve.

STRAWBERRY ICE CREAM

2 cups strawberries
¾ cup powdered sugar
2 egg whites, stiffly beaten
6 oz whipped cream or yoghurt
1 tsp vanilla

Crush strawberries. Add sugar, egg whites and vanilla. Mix well and carefully. Fold in whipped cream or yoghurt. Freeze.

STRAWBERRY PUDDING

½ lb strawberries
2 cups water
½ cup sugar
2 Tbs cornflour
2 egg whites

Reserve a few strawberries for decoration. Cook
the remaining strawberries in boiling water with ¼
cup sugar. Dilute cornflour with a little cold water,
add to strawberries and stir until thick. Pour into
stiffly beaten egg whites, beaten with ¼ cup sugar.
Mix gently and pour into individual dessert cups.
Chill.

STRAWBERRY MOUSSE

1 lb fresh strawberries, or
1 package frozen strawberries, thawed
juice of one lemon
½ cup sugar
2 packages instant strawberry jello mixed with 3
cups of liquid, one of which is the juice of the
strawberries
1 cup whipping cream, whipped
2 egg whites stiffly beaten

Cut strawberries in half, cover with lemon juice
and sugar. Set aside for 2 hours or overnight:
Drain liquid from strawberries. Prepare instant
jello with 2 cups of boiling water and 1 cup syrup
from strawberries. Pour over strawberries. When
cool, fold in whipped cream and egg whites.
Refrigerate for 2 hours before serving.

EQUIVALENTS

1 oz..	approx. 30 grams
1 lb	approx 454 grams
8 oz..	1 cup
1 cup	¼ litre
16 Tbs..	1 cup
4 Tbs..	¼ cup
1 quart	1.101 litre
1 pint	.551 litre
½ cup (butter or margarine)	approx. 120 grams
⅔ cup (butter or margarine)	approx. 160 grams
1¼ cup (butter or margarine)	approx. 300 grams

slow oven	268°F 131°C
moderate oven	350°F 177°C
hot oven	450°F−500°F 232°C−260°C

ABBREVIATIONS

Tb	Tablespoon
tsp	teaspoon
gr	gram
lb	pound
oz	ounce

INDEX

DATE DUE

~~MAR 1995~~			
~~APR 1995~~			

Demco, Inc. 38-293